BATTLE OF
GETTYSBURG

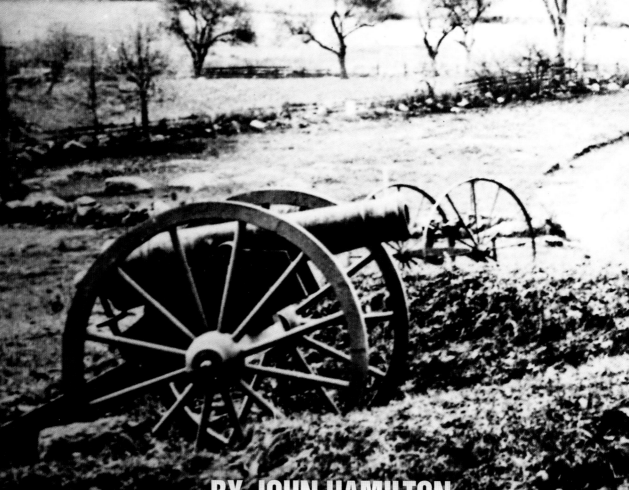

BY JOHN HAMILTON

VISIT US AT
WWW.ABDOPUBLISHING.COM

Published by ABDO Publishing Company, PO Box 398166, Minneapolis, MN 55439. Copyright ©2014 by Abdo Consulting Group, Inc. International copyrights reserved in all countries. No part of this book may be reproduced in any form without written permission from the publisher. ABDO & Daughters™ is a trademark and logo of ABDO Publishing Company.

Printed in the United States of America, North Mankato, Minnesota.
112013
012014

 PRINTED ON RECYCLED PAPER

Editor: Sue Hamilton
Graphic Design: John Hamilton
Cover Design: Neil Klinepier
Cover Photo: Emily Mitchell
Interior Photos and Illustrations: AP Images, p. 9 (Longstreet); Corbis, p. 13; Digital Stock, p. 1, 28 (corpses), 29; Getty Images, p. 5, 8, 16, 19, 24, 27, 28 (reenactor); Paintings by Don Troiani, www.historicalartprints.com, p. 18, 22, 23, 26; John Hamilton, p. 4, 11, 12, 14, 15, 17, 21, 25; Library of Congress, p. 6, 7, 9 (Lee), 10; Thinkstock, p. 20.

ABDO Booklinks
To learn more about Great Battles, visit ABDO Publishing Company online. Web sites about Great Battles are featured on our Booklinks pages. These links are routinely monitored and updated to provide the most current information available. Web site: www.abdopublishing.com

Library of Congress Control Number: 2013946967

Cataloging-in-Publication Data

Hamilton, John, 1959-
   Battle of Gettysburg / John Hamilton.
   p. cm. -- (Great battles)
Includes index.
ISBN 978-1-62403-203-5
1. Gettysburg, Battle of, Gettysburg, Pa., 1863--Juvenile literature.   I. Title.
973.7/349--dc23

2013946967

CONTENTS

A Nation Divided 4

Leaders of the Union 6

Leaders of the Confederacy 8

Lee's Northern Invasion 10

Tactics and Weapons 14

July 1, 1863: First Clash 16

July 2, 1863: Uphill Battle 20

July 3, 1863: Pickett's Charge 24

The Battle's Aftermath 28

Glossary 30

Index 32

A NATION DIVIDED

By the time Abraham Lincoln became president of the United States in March 1861, the nation had been torn in two. Eleven Southern states had seceded from the Union and formed the Confederate States of America. Their capital was in Richmond, Virginia, and Jefferson Davis was their president.

There were several causes of the Civil War, but slavery was the issue that most split the nation. President Lincoln waged war to abolish slavery and keep the Union intact.

The first two years favored the South. There were important Union victories, but the Confederates had a real chance of winning the war.

In June 1863, Confederate General Robert E. Lee executed a bold plan to invade the North. The result was the Battle of Gettysburg, the bloodiest battle ever fought on American soil, and a major turning point of the Civil War.

The Nation in 1861

- Union states
- Statehood 1863
- Confederate states
- Union states that allowed slavery
- Territories (present-day borders)

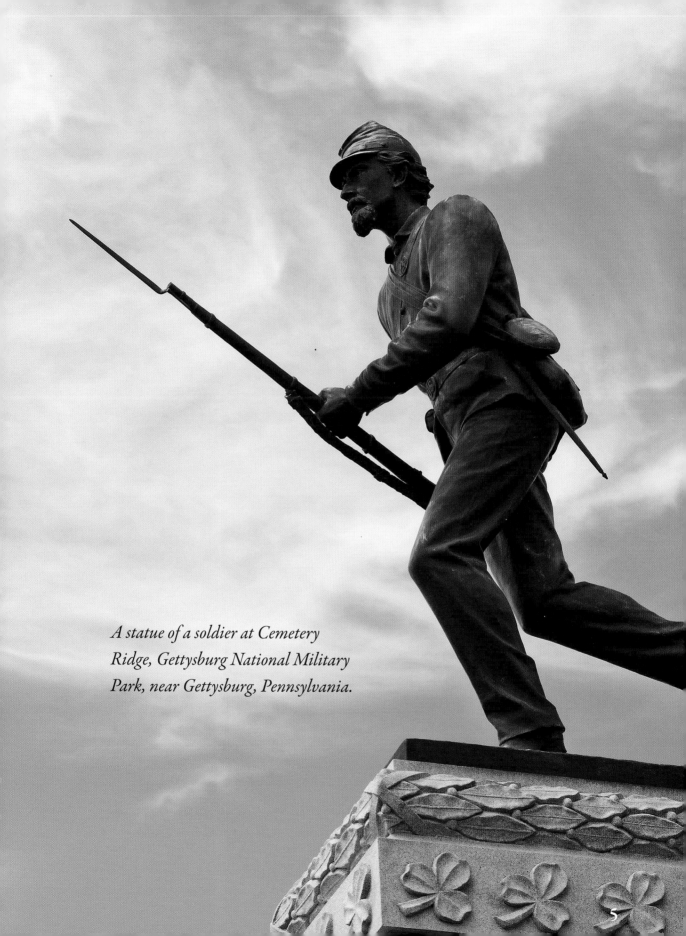

A statue of a soldier at Cemetery Ridge, Gettysburg National Military Park, near Gettysburg, Pennsylvania.

LEADERS OF THE UNION

President Abraham Lincoln (1809-1865) used his steady hand to guide the United States through the Civil War. Lincoln was intelligent and compassionate. He also had a unique way of motivating people with his uplifting speeches.

Born in Kentucky in 1809, Lincoln moved westward with his family, first to Indiana, then settling in Illinois. Mostly self-educated, he became a lawyer in 1836. Ten years later, he was elected to the U.S. House of Representatives. In March 1861, after winning election as an anti-slavery Republican, Lincoln took office as president of the United States, just as the country was plunged into its greatest crisis— the Civil War.

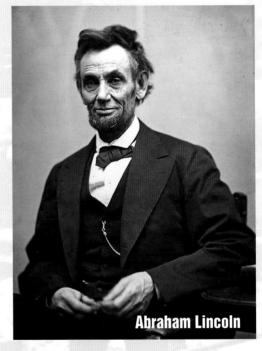

Abraham Lincoln

Southern states were tearing away from the United States, and Lincoln's job was to get them back to preserve the Union. The president balanced shrewd politics with deeply held moral beliefs, especially his anti-slavery stance. He was compassionate, yet he demanded results from those around him. As commander in chief of U.S. armed forces, Lincoln took an active role in war planning. He replaced his top generals several times, especially during the early war years when the Union suffered many losses.

By the time the Civil War ended in 1865, Lincoln had accomplished his goals of abolishing slavery and keeping the Union intact. Just days after the last major fighting of the war, an assassin's bullet struck the president. He died on April 15, 1865. Abraham Lincoln is remembered today as one of the greatest presidents in U.S. history.

Major General George Meade (1815-1872) guided Union forces during the Battle of Gettysburg. Meade took command of the Army of the Potomac just three days before

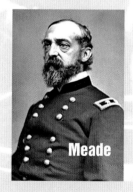

Meade

the battle began, replacing Major General Joseph Hooker. Meade was surprised that President Lincoln had given him such a responsibility, but he rose to the task. Nicknamed Old Snapping Turtle (because of his short temper), Meade had a reputation as a level-headed battlefield commander. He was neither rash nor timid. He was aggressive when the situation called for it, but he was also reluctant to send his troops into battle if the odds weren't in his favor.

Major General Winfield Hancock (1824-1886) took over as

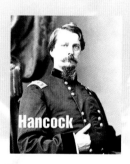

Hancock

corps commander at the Battle of Gettysburg after his superior, Major General John Reynolds, was killed in action. Hancock led the Union defenses on the first day of the battle. On the second and third day, as Union forces fought wave after wave of Confederate attacks, Hancock rallied his men and sent in reinforcements where they were needed the most. Hancock's bold leadership inspired his men.

LEADERS OF THE
CONFEDERACY

Jefferson Davis (1808-1889) was president of the Confederacy during the Civil War. Born in Kentucky in 1808, he trained as an Army officer at the United States Military Academy at West Point, New York. After serving in the Mexican-American War (1846-1848), Davis became the United States Secretary of War under President Franklin Pierce. He also served as U.S. senator for the state of Mississippi.

Jefferson Davis

Davis was a fierce supporter of the Southern states, and defended their right to use slaves. He was nominated in 1861 to become president of the breakaway Southern states, which called themselves the Confederate States of America. Duty bound, he accepted.

Davis wasn't as effective a leader as Abraham Lincoln. He was narrow-minded and stubborn. His staff and advisors constantly bickered, which made it difficult for him to make decisions. In addition, he was in a difficult position when it came to ordering the states to do what the newly formed government wanted. The entire Confederacy was founded on the idea that the states should be independent, so

Davis's decisions, even his command of the Confederate army, were viewed with suspicion.

After the South's surrender in 1865, Davis was captured and imprisoned without a trial for two years. Upon release, he moved to Canada. He later moved back to the United States and wrote a history of the Confederacy. Davis died in 1889, and is buried in Richmond, Virginia.

General Robert E. Lee (1807-1870) was the commander of the Confederate Army of Northern Virginia during the Civil War. He was the South's most successful and popular general. Lee was a military genius. Especially 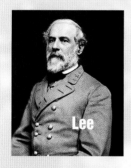 during the early years of the war, he managed to find ways to win battles, even against overwhelming odds.

Lee was born in Westmoreland County, Virginia, into a military family. He attended West Point, and spent many years as a U.S. Army officer, including service in the Mexican-American War. When the Civil War broke out, he was asked by President Lincoln to command the Union army. Lee didn't approve of slavery or the Southern states's secession, but he couldn't bring himself to fight against his beloved home state of Virginia. Instead, he left the U.S. Army and became a general with the Confederates.

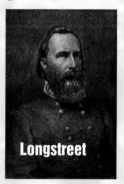

Longstreet

General James Longstreet was one of General Robert E. Lee's most trusted corps commanders. Lee called him "Old War Horse." During the Battle of Gettysburg, Longstreet and Lee disagreed about the wisdom of attacking the Union's defensive positions on July 3, 1863, the final day of the battle. Longstreet feared the attack would result in massive casualties among his men, which in fact did occur. Afterwards, Longstreet was criticized for taking too long to launch the assault.

LEE'S NORTHERN
INVASION

During the first two years of the Civil War, the Confederacy won many battlefield victories. General Robert E. Lee and his Army of Northern Virginia always seemed to find a way to win, even against overwhelming odds. By 1863, Lee and his officers remained confident.

Confederate troops

But the war had taken its toll on the South, where most of the fighting had taken place. Thousands of soldiers were dead, wounded, or captured, and many Southern cities were in ruins. Supply shortages had reached critical levels. Lee wanted to end the war as quickly as possible. His plan: invade the North.

General Lee had tried once already, in 1862, to invade Northern lands. Maryland's Battle of Antietam ended in a draw, but Lee's army was forced to retreat back to Virginia. Now, less than one year later, Lee wanted to try again. He convinced Confederate President Jefferson Davis that invading the North would accomplish several goals. Lee's army could raid the supplies of the rich agricultural

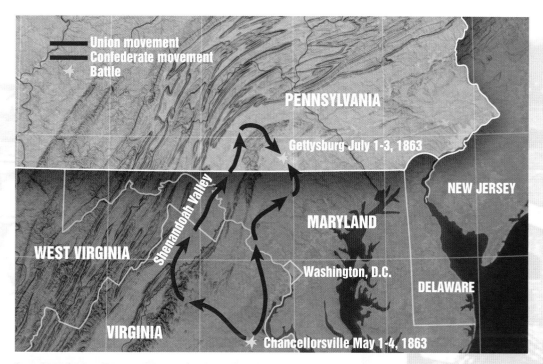

Union movement
Confederate movement
★ Battle

PENNSYLVANIA

Gettysburg July 1-3, 1863

NEW JERSEY

Shenandoah Valley

MARYLAND

WEST VIRGINIA

Washington, D.C.

DELAWARE

VIRGINIA

★ Chancellorsville May 1-4, 1863

lands of southern Pennsylvania. Lee also hoped the invasion would fuel a growing anti-war movement in the North. There were many who wanted peace with the Confederacy, even if it meant giving the South its independence. Lee thought his invasion plan would put even more pressure on President Abraham Lincoln to stop the war.

Lee also believed that a successful invasion would draw support from possible overseas allies, such as Great Britain or France. These allies could give the South much-needed supplies and weapons.

By threatening Northern cities, especially Philadelphia, Pennsylvania, and Washington, D.C., Lee hoped to force the North to pull troops away from other critical battlefields, such as the forces under the command of General Ulysses S. Grant. Union troops at that time were threatening Vicksburg, Mississippi, the last Confederate stronghold on the Mississippi River.

Most importantly, General Robert E. Lee didn't want to simply win a battle in the North. He wanted to win the Civil War with one final, crushing victory.

On June 3, about a month after winning a major battle at Chancellorsville, Virginia, Lee's forces headed west, crossed a narrow stretch of mountains, and then marched north, up the Shenandoah Valley. By late June, the 72,000-man army had crossed West Virginia and moved into southern Pennsylvania.

The Confederates traveled through lands that were yet untouched by the war. As they marched from town to town, they raided much-needed supplies, including food, clothing, and shoes. General Lee made sure that the rightful owners were properly paid—in Confederate money. The people whose property was taken were unimpressed. Confederate money had little value to Northerners, and it became totally worthless after the South later lost the war in 1865.

As Lee's forces moved into Pennsylvania, the Union's Army of the Potomac tracked the Confederates, moving parallel to the enemy in a northward direction. The Union forces acted as a shield, keeping themselves between the enemy and Washington, D.C. The Union army, about 94,000 strong, was led by General Joseph Hooker, the commander who had lost the Battle of Chancellorsville.

General Hooker and President Lincoln quarreled often. At one point, Hooker demanded extra

Union troops on the move.

The little town of Gettysburg, Pennsylvania, just before the battle.

troops and offered to resign if he didn't get his way. Lincoln eagerly accepted Hooker's resignation and replaced him with 47-year-old General George Meade. General Meade took command of the Union army on June 28, just three days before the Battle of Gettysburg.

President Lincoln's orders to Meade were simple, but difficult: protect Washington, D.C., at all costs, and seek out and destroy the Army of Northern Virginia.

These two huge armies, the Union Army of the Potomac and the Confederate Army of Northern Virginia, moved along the area's roadways. With thousands of soldiers, wagons, and equipment

to transport, roads were the best way to move rapidly. The army that controlled the major road junctions had the best chance of winning battles.

The tiny town of Gettysburg, population about 2,000, had 10 roads leading into it. It was like the center of a wheel with lots of spokes pointing into town. It was a vital road junction that both sides wanted to control. By the end of June, the two sides found themselves drawing closer and closer to each other. Lee's invasion of the North was about to spark a three-day clash at Gettysburg, one of the largest battles in United States history.

TACTICS AND WEAPONS

The most common infantry weapon in 1863 was the single-shot, muzzle-loading rifled musket. Experienced Union and Confederate soldiers could load and fire their American-made Springfields and English-made Enfields three-to-four times per minute. The inside of the barrel was grooved, not smooth. This caused minie ball ammunition to spin, resulting in accurate strikes up to 250 yards (229 m) away.

Cavalrymen carried Sharps and Burnside carbines. Their light weight and short barrels made them easier to handle on horseback. Cavalrymen also carried knives, swords, and sabers.

The most common Civil War artillery piece was the smoothbore, 12-pound Napoleon cannon, but many other types of cannons and howitzers were also used. Artillery was effective against targets almost one mile (1.6 km) away.

Union reenactors line up against Confederate artillery.

Unfortunately, Civil War battlefield commanders did not keep up with their weapons's deadly accuracy. Generals still used tactics from the Napoleon Bonaparte era of the late 1700s and early 1800s. Soldiers stood shoulder-to-shoulder in two or three long lines, one in back of the other. They marched in the open toward the enemy, fired their rifles simultaneously, and then charged with their rifle-mounted bayonets. However, against the more accurate weapons of the mid-1800's, Civil War soldiers often faced almost certain death or injury.

Union infantry with rifled muskets and bayonets.

Minie balls

Artillery could fire exploding cannon balls, or cannister shot, which was especially deadly against enemy troops.

15

JULY 1, 1863
FIRST CLASH

The Battle of Gettysburg was fought over three long, hot days in July, 1863. Though often overlooked, the first day's fighting was filled with savage struggles, raw courage, tragedy, and desperate hope.

A famous story says that the battle began because a Confederate patrol came to Gettysburg seeking shoes for the troops. That story is almost certainly not true. (For one thing, there was no shoe factory in the town.) Instead, on the morning of July 1, 1863, Confederate Major General Henry Heth led his 7,000-man infantry division toward Gettysburg, looking for a fight. The Confederates knew that Union forces were somewhere in the vicinity. General Lee, commander of the Army of Northern Virginia,

Union cavalry reenactors battle Confederate infantry.

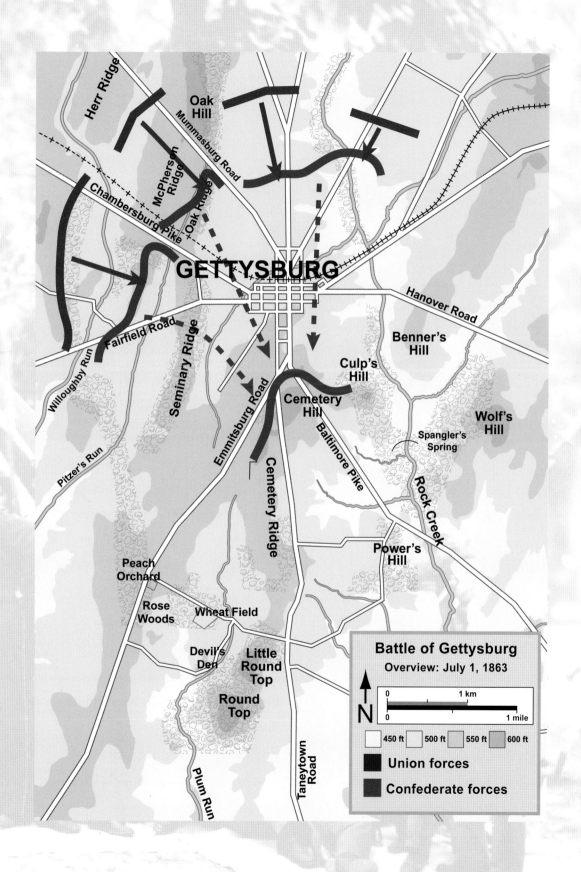

Soldiers of the 6th Wisconsin Iron Brigade struggle for the colors of the 2nd Mississippi.

gave orders not to engage the enemy until his entire army could gather. General Heth pressed forward anyway, eager to fight the Yankees.

The battle began just north and west of the town. At 5:30 am, Lieutenant Marcellus E. Jones of the 8th Illinois Cavalry saw the shadows of a Confederate cavalry patrol in the distance. Jones fired a shot with his carbine rifle, then hurried away to raise the alarm.

Both sides began pouring into the area and lining up against one another.

Reinforcements were hurriedly sent for. The first skirmish was between Union Brigadier General John Buford's cavalry and the infantry of Confederate Major General Henry Heth. The Yankees dismounted and held the line as they awaited reinforcements. Just in the nick of time, Major General John Reynolds's First Corps arrived to strengthen Buford's position.

Reynolds' men included crack troops from the "Iron Brigade," a group made up of rugged volunteers from Wisconsin, Indiana, and Michigan. Known for their black Hardee hats and fierce fighting style, they sent Heth's rebels reeling back. Many Confederates were killed, wounded, or captured. The Iron Brigade, too, suffered many casualties, but they bought precious time for the Union side.

Just south of Gettysburg, Union troops under the command of Major General Oliver Howard worked feverishly to set up fortifications and trenches along Cemetery Hill and Culp's Hill, which had commanding views of the area. With properly set up defenses at these spots, Union forces would be very hard to defeat.

Meanwhile, west of town, Union General Reynolds ordered a Wisconsin regiment to attack, but was then shot in the back of the neck. He died just as the battle began to intensify.

Troops from both sides poured into the Gettysburg area. Approximately 18,000 Union troops fought 30,000 Confederates. The Union side held on until afternoon, when repeated Confederate attacks became overwhelming. The Union line collapsed, and troops fled south. Many escaped to the heights south of Gettysburg. Others were trapped and killed in the streets of the town.

The cost of the first day's battle was great—9,000 Union and 7,000 Confederate casualties. But the Union troops's brave defense worked: Meade's army now occupied the high ground. They would sorely need it. The day's fighting was one of the bloodiest of the war, but there was worse to come.

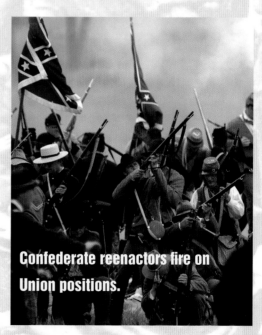

Confederate reenactors fire on Union positions.

JULY 2, 1863
UPHILL BATTLE

At dawn on July 2, 1863, the second day of the battle, Confederate General Robert E. Lee assessed his situation. He rode his horse along the rebel position at Seminary Ridge, southwest of Gettysburg. Confederate forces, about 70,000 strong, faced off against 90,000 Union troops.

Union forces occupied the high ground south of Gettysburg, on Cemetery Hill and Culp's Hill. They were also strung out southward along Cemetery Ridge. The entire Union line resembled a giant fishhook. Union General Meade could easily send reinforcements anywhere Lee's forces attacked.

A statue of Union General Kemble Warren on Little Round Top, overlooking the area around Gettysburg.

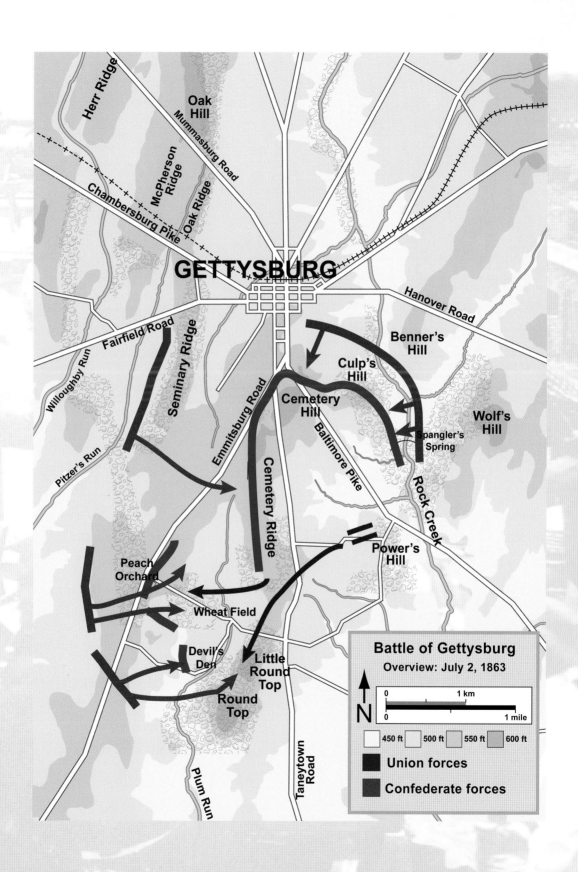

Herr Ridge

Oak Hill

McPherson Ridge

Mummasburg Road

Oak Ridge

Chambersburg Pike

GETTYSBURG

Hanover Road

Fairfield Road

Seminary Ridge

Willoughby Run

Pitzer's Run

Emmitsburg Road

Cemetery Hill

Culp's Hill

Benner's Hill

Wolf's Hill

Spangler's Spring

Cemetery Ridge

Baltimore Pike

Rock Creek

Power's Hill

Peach Orchard

Wheat Field

Devil's Den

Little Round Top

Round Top

Plum Run

Taneytown Road

Battle of Gettysburg

Overview: July 2, 1863

N

0   1 km

0   1 mile

450 ft   500 ft   550 ft   600 ft

Union forces

Confederate forces

21

Union troops of the 20th Maine, led by Colonel Joshua Chamberlain, swoop down with bayonets upon a unit of Alabama soldiers attacking Little Round Top.

That afternoon, on one of the hottest days of the year, Lee launched an assault against the Union's left side (left flank). Under the command of Lieutenant General James Longstreet, tens of thousands of rebels struck. Savage fighting broke out in such places as Devil's Den, the Wheat Field, the Peach Orchard, and along Cemetery Ridge.

Along the center of the Union line, a bulge developed when General Daniel Sickles moved his artillery units far forward of where they were supposed to be stationed.

His men were soon attacked. The Union sent reinforcements as Sickles's men fought for their lives. These reinforcements, however, left a gaping hole in the Union line along Cemetery Ridge. The rebels were quick to take advantage, sending a massive wave of men forward, hoping to split the Union army in two.

Fresh Union reinforcements rushed to fill the gap, but they weren't fast enough. A group of 262 soldiers from the 1st Minnesota Regiment delayed the rebels just long enough

Bloody hand-to-hand combat in the Wheat Field. Control of the area changed hands several times before the Confederates finally drove off Union soldiers.

for reinforcements to arrive, but at a terrible cost—82 percent of the regiment were killed or wounded.

On the Union's far left side, at a high point called Little Round Top, a rebel assault almost succeeded. It could have been a disaster for the Union. Confederate control of such an important spot might have forced the entire Union army to retreat. Luckily, thanks to the efforts of men from the 20th Maine Regiment, plus newly arrived reinforcements, the Union

continued to hold on to Little Round Top. The 20th Maine lost 130 of its 386 men, but the exhausted rebels withdrew.

A Confederate attack later that evening on the Union's right flank, atop Culp's Hill and Cemetery Hill, was equally fierce. The rebels captured a few positions, but the dug-in Union troops for the most part held onto the important high ground. Lee's attacks on the Union flanks had failed. But he would try again the following day.

JULY 3, 1863
PICKETT'S CHARGE

In the pre-dawn hours of July 3, 1863, the third and final day of the Battle of Gettysburg, Confederate forces planned once more to take Culp's Hill, the high ground on the Union's right flank. Union forces struck first, bombarding the rebels with artillery fire, then engaging them in vicious combat. For several hours, the Confederates rallied and charged again and again, but were beaten back each time. Finally, the rebels gave up all hope of taking the hill.

Union reenactors fire a volley toward Confederate troops.

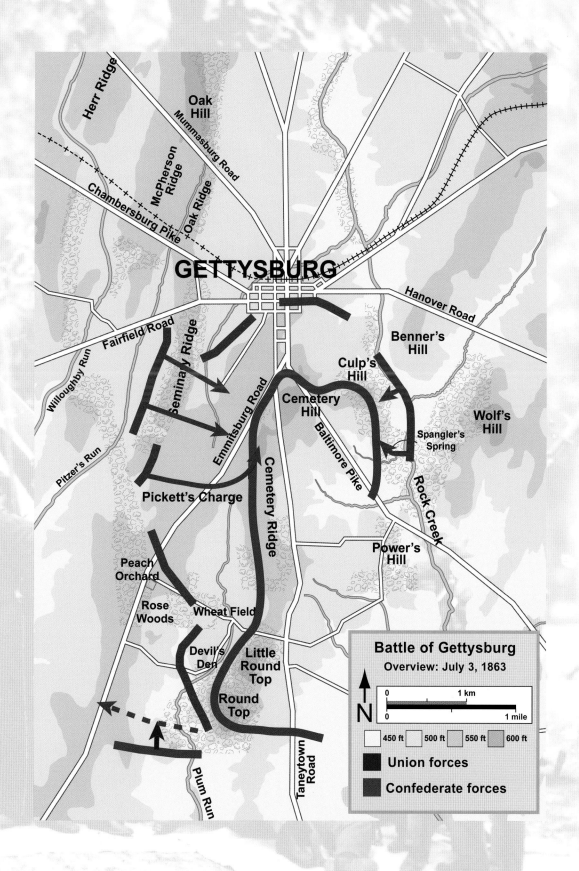

Herr Ridge

Oak Hill

Mummasburg Road

McPherson Ridge

Oak Ridge

Chambersburg Pike

GETTYSBURG

Hanover Road

Fairfield Road

Seminary Ridge

Benner's Hill

Culp's Hill

Willoughby Run

Emmitsburg Road

Cemetery Hill

Baltimore Pike

Wolf's Hill

Spangler's Spring

Pitzer's Run

Rock Creek

Pickett's Charge

Cemetery Ridge

Power's Hill

Peach Orchard

Rose Woods

Wheat Field

Devil's Den

Little Round Top

Round Top

Plum Run

Taneytown Road

Battle of Gettysburg

Overview: July 3, 1863

N

| 0 | | 1 km | |
| 0 | | | 1 mile |

450 ft   500 ft   550 ft   600 ft

Union forces

Confederate forces

Led by General Lewis Armistead, Confederates try to break the Union center line at Cemetery Ridge.

Confederate General Robert E. Lee, frustrated in his failed plan to attack the enemy's flanks, decided to launch an all-out, frontal infantry assault on the Union center line atop Cemetery Ridge. It was a bold plan, filled with peril.

Confederate Lieutenant General James Longstreet feared that a frontal assault against dug-in Union troops on high ground would only result in fearful Confederate losses. He told General Lee that, in his opinion, the rebel army should move southeast, to the Union army's right. They could then fortify their position and await a Union attack, which would give the rebels better odds. The Confederates could even move farther south and threaten Washington, D.C.

General Lee quickly put an end to such talk. "The enemy is there," he said, pointing toward the Union line on the ridge, "and I am going to strike him." Lee's mind was made up. He had absolute confidence in his soldiers. "They will go anywhere and do anything," Lee once said, "if properly led."

At 1:00 pm, more than 150 Confederate cannons opened fire in an attempt to weaken the Union troops on Cemetery Ridge. Union cannons returned fire. At 3:30 pm, about 12,500 troops, including fresh Confederates under the command of General George Pickett, left the cover of the woods and set out across almost one mile (1.6 km) of open field, steadily marching up a gentle slope toward the enemy-occupied ridge. They faced murderous cannon and rifle fire from the Union side. The withering attack was devastating. Still, the courageous Confederates marched on. With a rebel yell that sent tremors through the Union ranks, they charged the enemy. At one point, they almost broke through, but the Union troops held firm. After furious hand-to-hand combat, the rebels were driven back.

As fighting raged on Cemetery Ridge, Confederate cavalry under the command of Major General "Jeb" Stuart clashed with Union cavalry three miles (5 km) east of

A clash of cavalry.

Gettysburg. Stuart's aim was to attack the Union from behind and cut off its supplies. If the plan had worked, it might have won the entire battle. But Union cavalry, some led by a young General George Armstrong Custer, beat back the rebels with carbines and sabers.

"Pickett's Charge" was a disaster for the Confederates. Almost half of Pickett's men were either killed, wounded, or captured. Thousands of corpses littered the battlefield. Ordered by General Lee to prepare for a possible Union counterattack, General Pickett replied, "General Lee, I have no division now."

A dejected General Lee rode out to greet his battered men. "All this has been my fault," he said. The day, and the Battle of Gettysburg, had been lost.

THE BATTLE'S
AFTERMATH

ettysburg was the bloodiest single battle ever fought on American soil. During three days of desperate fighting, approximately 28,000 Confederate troops were either killed, wounded, or captured, almost 40 percent of the rebels who had fought. More than 23,000 Union troops were also lost in battle, a casualty rate of 25 percent.

Confederate General Lee, his Army of Northern Virginia badly broken, ordered a withdrawal from the Gettysburg area. Over the next several days, he led the retreat through a miserable rain. The wounded, carried in springless wagons, cried out with every bump in the rutted roads. Finally, by July 14, 1863, the last of Lee's forces

A Union reenactor carries a war-torn U.S. flag.

Corpses litter a field at Gettysburg in July 1863.

crossed the Potomac River back into Confederate territory in Virginia.

Union General George Meade was later criticized for not pursuing Lee and crushing the Southern army once and for all. Meade, however, became cautious. His own army was battered and bruised, and he had little desire to force another major battle so soon after Gettysburg.

For days and weeks after the battle, the grounds around Gettysburg were strewn with thousands of Union and Confederate dead. Bodies lay scattered in ditches or on farmlands. Many were hastily buried in shallow graves to prevent the spread of disease.

Later, Gettysburg National Cemetery was built as a final resting place for the Union dead. (Most of the Confederate dead were moved to cemeteries in the South.)

At the cemetery's dedication ceremony on November 19, 1863, President Lincoln gave a brief, two-minute speech called the Gettysburg Address. It became one of the most famous speeches in American history. Lincoln talked

President Lincoln delivering the Gettysburg Address on November 19, 1863.

about the soldiers who had died at Gettysburg, and the nation's need to honor their sacrifice by continuing the long struggle for freedom for all Americans.

The Union victory at Gettysburg gave hope to Northerners that Robert E. Lee's forces were not invincible, and that the Union army could actually win the Civil War. There would be almost two long years of bloodshed yet to endure, until the South finally surrendered in April 1865. But the Battle of Gettysburg, at least, had turned the tide of the war in the Union's favor.

GLOSSARY

ARMY OF THE POTOMAC
The main Union army of the eastern United States, named after the Potomac River. Responsible for protecting Washington, D.C., it fought mainly in eastern Virginia, Maryland, and Pennsylvania.

CANNISTER SHOT
A kind of ammunition used in cannons. Large iron balls are packed into a cylindrical cannister, which is then shot out of the cannon. The cannister splits apart, sending the balls in an outward-spreading pattern, like a shotgun. Cannister shot is particularly deadly against groups of soldiers.

CEMETERY HILL
The northern part of Cemetery Ridge, just south of the town of Gettysburg. The hill, a line of high ground that runs north and south, was held by Union troops during the Battle of Gettysburg. It is named after Evergreen Cemetery, which was used by the town several years before the battle.

CIVIL WAR
A war where two parts of the same nation fight against each other. The American Civil War was fought between Northern and Southern states from 1861–1865. The Southern states were for slavery. They wanted to start their own country. Northern states fought against slavery and a division of the country.

CONFEDERACY

The Southern states of Alabama, Arkansas, Florida, Georgia, Louisiana, Mississippi, North Carolina, South Carolina, Tennessee, Texas, and Virginia. These states wanted to keep slavery legal. They broke away from the United States during the Civil War and formed their own country known as the Confederate States of America. The Confederacy ended in 1865 when the war ended and the 11 Confederate states rejoined the United States.

HOWITZER

An artillery piece that fires relatively slow-moving shells in high arcs toward the target. The explosive shells rain down on the enemy, almost like bombs dropped from an airplane. Howitzers are useful for attacking enemy forces that are sheltered behind hills or trenches. This type of artillery attack is called indirect fire.

NAPOLEON CANNON

Developed by the French in the 1850s, smoothbore Napoleon cannons became very popular by the world's armies because of their reliability and close-range killing power. They were used extensively by both the Union and Confederate armies in the American Civil War.

REINFORCEMENTS

Extra soldiers that are sent to support (reinforce) the strength of an army. Having fresh reinforcements available can be critical to winning battles.

UNION

The Northern states united against the Confederacy. "Union" also refers to all of the states of the United States. President Lincoln wanted to preserve the Union, keeping the Northern and Southern states together.

INDEX

A

Antietam, Battle of 10
Army, U.S. 9
Army of Northern Virginia 9, 10, 13, 16, 28
Army of the Potomac 7, 12, 13

B

Bonaparte, Napoleon 15
Buford, John 18

C

Canada 9
Cemetery Hill 19, 20, 23
Cemetery Ridge 20, 22, 26, 27
Chancellorsville, VA 12
Chancellorsville, Battle of 12
Civil War 4, 6, 7, 8, 9, 10, 11, 14, 15, 29
Confederacy (*see* Confederate States of America)
Confederate States of America 4, 8, 9, 10, 11, 12, 13, 14, 16, 18, 19, 23, 24, 26, 26, 28, 29
Culp's Hill 19, 20, 23, 24
Custer, George Armstrong 27

D

Davis, Jefferson 4, 8, 9, 10
Devil's Den 22

E

8th Illinois Cavalry 18

F

First Corps, Union 18
1st Minnesota Regiment 22
France 11

G

Gettysburg, PA 13, 16, 19, 20, 27, 28, 29
Gettysburg Address 29

Gettysburg National Cemetery 29
Grant, Ulysses S. 11
Great Britain 11

H

Hancock, Winfield 7
Heth, Henry 16, 18, 19
Hooker, Joseph 7, 12, 13
House of Representatives, U.S. 6
Howard, Oliver 19

I

Illinois 6
Indiana 6, 19
Iron Brigade 18, 19

J

Jones, Marcellus E. 18

K

Kentucky 6, 8

L

Lee, Robert E. 4, 9, 10, 11, 12, 13, 16, 20, 22, 23, 26, 27, 28, 29
Lincoln, Abraham 4, 6, 7, 8, 9, 11, 12, 13, 29
Little Round Top 23
Longstreet, James 9, 22, 26

M

Maryland 10
Meade, George 7, 13, 19, 20, 29
Mexican-American War 8, 9
Michigan 19
Mississippi River 11

N

North 4, 10, 11, 13

P

Peach Orchard 22
Pennsylvania 11
Philadelphia, PA 11
Pickett, George 27
Pickett's Charge 27
Pierce, Franklin 8
Potomac River 29

R

Reynolds, John 7, 18, 19
Richmond, VA 4, 9

S

Seminary Ridge 20
Shenandoah Valley 12
Sickles, Daniel 22
South 4, 9, 10, 11
Stuart, Jeb 27

T

20th Maine Regiment 23

U

Union 4, 6, 7, 9, 11, 12, 13, 14, 16, 18, 19, 22, 23, 24, 26, 27, 29
United States 4, 6, 8, 9, 13
United States Military Academy (*see also* West Point, NY) 8, 9

V

Vicksburg, MS 11
Virginia 9, 10

W

Washington, D.C. 11, 12, 13, 26
West Point, NY 8, 9
West Virginia 12
Westmoreland County, VA 9
Wheat Field 22
Wisconsin 19